Contents

Acknowledgments

The Central Office of Information would like to thank the Department for Education, the Welsh Office, The Scottish Office and the Department of Education for Northern Ireland for their co-operation in compiling this book.

Cover Photograph Credit

Courtesy of the Northern Ireland Centre for Learning Resources.

Introduction

Parents are required by law to see that their children receive full-time education, at school or elsewhere, between the ages of 5 and 16 in England, Scotland and Wales and 4 and 16 in Northern Ireland. Some 9 million children attend Britain's 34,800 state[1] and independent schools.

About 93 per cent of pupils receive free education in state schools, while the others attend independent schools which are financed from fees paid by parents.

This book describes recent educational reforms in England and Wales, including increased rights for parents; the National Curriculum; new school inspection systems; and the efforts being made to relate teacher training more closely to the needs of the classroom.

The purpose of the reforms is to make schools more accountable for the education they offer to their pupils. Their main features are:

—National Curriculum targets enabling pupils' progress to be judged by parents and schools;

—assessment arrangements in the core subjects of English, mathematics and science, and public examinations which measure pupils' progress;

—publication of the results of National Curriculum tests and public examinations, backed up by regular independent school

---

[1]For ease of reference the term 'state school' is used to describe schools financed from public funds.

inspections designed to enable parents to hold schools to account for their performance; and

—greater autonomy for school governing bodies.

Similar reforms have also taken place in Scottish and Northern Irish schools. Since there are some important differences in organisation and practice, the book has separate sections dealing with the school education systems in England and Wales, Scotland and Northern Ireland.

England and Wales

The Department for Education, headed by the Secretary of State for Education, has overall responsibility for school education in England. The Welsh Office Education Department and the Secretary of State for Wales are responsible for the education system in Wales. There are three kinds of state school:

—county schools owned and maintained by local education authorities (LEAs) from public funds;

—voluntary aided and voluntary controlled schools, which were largely established by churches: they, too, are maintained from public funds, although the governors of voluntary aided schools do contribute to capital costs; and

—self-governing grant-maintained (GM) schools, which have opted out of LEA control following a ballot of parents (see p. 13).

Parental Rights

School Admissions

Although parents have the statutory right to choose a school for their children, this choice cannot always be met since the school may be full of pupils with a stronger claim. Most children are offered places at their parents' first choice of school. There are published admissions criteria which are available at least six weeks before parents can apply for places for their children. The criteria must be clear and easy to understand.

Decisions on admissions are taken by the local authority in the case of LEA schools. Governors of GM schools or of voluntary aided schools are responsible for admitting children to their schools. Under the 1993 Education Act, the Secretary of State has a reserve power to direct LEAs and GM state schools to co-ordinate their admission arrangements if they cannot reach agreement at local level.

The admission authorities are required by law to admit children on demand in order to meet fully the physical capacity of the school. This helps to maximise parents' chances of obtaining a place for their child at their preferred school. Priority may be given to children with brothers or sisters in the school or who live in a clearly defined catchment area.

If parents do not obtain their choice of school, they have the right to appeal to an independent committee. If the committee rules in the parents' favour, the child must be admitted to the school. Under the 1993 Education Act, all admission appeal committees will have to contain a lay independent member, as well as those appointed by either the LEA or the governing body.

If parents feel that the appeal is not handled properly by the committee, they can complain to the Local Government Ombudsman. The Ombudsman's power is being extended to cover GM schools.

School Information for Parents

Information about a school is published in a prospectus for the use of parents. This provides details about the organisation of teaching, public examination results, National Curriculum assessment results (see p. 24), attendance figures, admission policy and school uniform policy.

State schools have to give parents a written report each year on the education of their child. Reports must contain a summary of the pupil's progress in school curriculum subjects, including the results of assessment tests in the core subjects of English, mathematics and science (see p. 22) and details about qualifications achieved from taking public examinations. This takes the form of a short commentary on progress, highlighting strengths and achievements and identifying any particular weaknesses, together with suggestions for positive future action. Information about qualifications gained should include details of vocational qualifications or credits towards such qualifications. Schools are also required to include comparative information about National Curriculum assessment and examination results of pupils of the same age.

In addition, reports must:

— set out details of attendance record and general progress, including contributions to the life of the school and any special achievements during the year; and

— include information about arrangements for discussing the report with teachers.

The school governors must provide an annual report to parents about the school, its finances, any changes in the school prospectus and information about the governors' work to strengthen the school's links with the community, including the police. It must also contain information about the date, time and place of the annual parents' meeting (see p. 6).

Governors are expected to consider whether, given the ethnic make-up of the community served by the school, the prospectus and other documents should be translated into other languages.

National comparative tables are published on state and independent secondary school performance, including details about examination results and information about vocational qualifications and unauthorised absence by pupils. Head teachers are required to provide a report on their school achievements to school leavers. The report must include information about:

—the subject and attainment levels of every National Curriculum subject studied;

—the results of any public examinations, qualifications achieved and credits gained; and

—brief particulars of achievements in all subjects and activities studied as part of the school curriculum during the last year of study in the school.

The National Record of Achievement is used as a means of providing leavers with this mandatory report on their school attainments.

If a pupil transfers to another school, a record of his or her accomplishments is sent to the new school.

Annual Parents' Meeting

All parents have to be invited to the annual parents' meeting, which is held to enable parents to discuss with the governors and the head teacher what has been happening in the school over the past year. This involves discussion of the governors' annual school report and any matters raised by parents about the running of the school.

School Inspections

Under the new system of school inspections (see p. 29), parents are sent a readable summary of the full inspection report, which is published. School governors have to prepare action plans to follow it up and then report back to parents regularly on the progress made in carrying out its recommendations.

Children with Special Educational Needs

Special educational needs (SENs) comprise learning difficulties of all kinds, including mental or physical disabilities which hinder or prevent learning.

Under the 1993 Education Act, which builds on and largely replaces previous legislation, a Code of Practice has been issued by the Secretary of State and approved by Parliament. The Code gives practical guidance on how to identify and assess special educational needs, and comes into force on 1 September 1994. All schools and LEAs must consult the Code when dealing with children with special educational needs.

The Code recommends that schools adopt a staged model when dealing with SEN children:

Stage 1—Class or subject teachers identify or register a child's needs and, consulting the teacher responsible for co-ordinating SEN provision within the school, take initial action and talk to parents.

Stage 2—The SEN co-ordinator talks to parents and teachers and draws up an individual education plan setting out targets for the child to achieve.

Stage 3—If the child requires more help, the school looks for specialist assistance or advice from outside the school. Teachers and the outside specialist draw up a new individual education plan for the pupil.

Although most children's needs will by now have been met by the school, perhaps one child in every 50 will require extra assistance. In such cases, the head teacher will decide whether to ask the LEA to make a statutory assessment, which is a detailed examination designed to discover the educational needs of the pupil.

Parents are always consulted before the request is made. They can also ask the LEA for an assessment.

If the LEA goes ahead with an assessment, it must inform the parents, who are asked to provide information and give their views about the child's needs. Parents have the right to go with their child to any interview or medical test during the assessment. The views of the child about his or her needs may be sought by the LEA. In addition, independent advice is available to parents through a named person who may come from a voluntary organisation or parents' support group or be a professional, friend or relative.

Once the LEA has collected all the advice and comments about the child's needs, it decides whether to make a statement setting out the child's educational needs and the special help he or she should have. Parents are given the opportunity to give their views on the statement before it is finalised. The normal statutory timetable from proposing an assessment to making a statement is six months.

The child's statement has to be reviewed annually by the LEA in order to ensure that it continues to meet his or her needs. Parents are entitled to be present at the review meeting, which is normally held in the child's school. The child can also be present for part of the meeting to put forward his or her views on progress made. Parents are always asked to give their views if any changes to the statement are made.

If parents disagree with any LEA decisions, they can, from September 1994, appeal to the Special Educational Needs Tribunal, which is an independent body. The Tribunal Chairman is a lawyer and the other two members have experience of special educational needs and local government. Appeals may be made to the Tribunal if:

—the LEA refuses to make a statutory assessment of a child when asked by the parents to do so; or

—the LEA refuses to make a statement after an assessment; or

—the parents disagree with parts of the statement; or

—the child has a statement and the LEA refuses to re-assess the child again or change the name of the school in the statement; or

—the LEA decides to stop keeping the statement up-to-date.

Parents can attend Tribunal hearings and can ask up to two professionals who know the child to speak on their behalf. The Tribunal considers all the evidence and takes a final decision on the case. Applications to the Tribunal must be made no later than two months after the LEA's decision.

Most SEN children are educated in ordinary schools, while others go to special schools. All children in special schools normally have statements or are undergoing assessment. Parents have the right to express a preference for the state school they want their child to go to. The LEA has to agree with this provided that:

—the school chosen is suitable for the child's age, ability and special educational needs;

—the child's presence does not affect the efficient education of other pupils at the school; and

—the placement of the child is an efficient use of the LEA's resources.

From September 1994, schools must publish information about, and report on, the school's policy on special educational needs. This includes basic information, such as the name of the school's SEN co-ordinator, admission arrangements and facilities for pupils. Information must be provided about the school's arrangements for deciding which pupils need special help and their plans for giving that assistance. In addition, details must be given on the school's staffing policies, its partnership with parents and its links with outside agencies, such as health and social services and voluntary bodies.

Local School Management

LEA schools have a governing body consisting of representatives from parents of the school's children, teachers at the school, people appointed by the LEA, business people and others working in the local community. Parent governors are elected by parents of registered pupils at the school and serve for a period of four years. Teacher governors are elected by, and from among, the teachers at the school. The LEA is responsible for conducting parent and teacher governor elections. The head teacher can choose whether or not to be a member of the governing body and in any case has the right to attend all its meetings. The co-opted members are chosen by the parent, teacher and LEA governors from the local community, including business interests.

The 75,000 parent governors have a close interest in improving the quality of their local school for the benefit of their own children and those of the parents they represent. About 20 per cent of governors come from a business background; many large employers allow employees time off to attend those governors' meetings which take place in working time.

The school governing body must meet at least once in every term. Minutes recording the proceedings are available at the school for anyone wanting to inspect them, unless there are some confidential details concerning an individual pupil or member of staff.

Under legislation passed in 1986 governing bodies:

—are responsible for the general conduct of the school;

—must consider the curriculum for the school;

—may offer the head teacher general principles to follow in determining policy on school discipline;

—have control over money given to them by the local authority to cover expenditure on books, equipment and stationery;

—may take part in procedures for selecting the school's staff;

—must make information about the school available to parents; and

—are responsible for preparing an annual report to parents and holding an annual meeting with them to discuss it and any other matters concerning the running of the school.

Under the 1988 Education Reform Act, which gave governors important new powers and duties, governors share responsibility with the LEA and the head teacher for ensuring that:

—the school curriculum is broad and balanced and meets the requirements of the National Curriculum;

—courses leading to public examinations for pupils of compulsory school age are for approved qualifications and follow approved syllabuses;

—the law on religious education and collective worship is complied with; and

—information about the curriculum and pupils' achievements is given to parents.

Financial Delegation

The 1988 Act provides for financial delegation to be made to schools by the LEA. By April 1994 financial delegation was phased in to all secondary and primary schools (1995 for all primary schools in Wales). Local authorities will be able to delegate budgets to special schools if they so wish.

The aim is to devolve as many decisions as possible to schools by shifting resources from central administration to school budgets managed by governors and head teachers.

LEAs are required to delegate 85 per cent of the potential schools' budget. In addition 80 per cent of the sum delegated is directly related to the number and age of their pupils. So, if a school is popular with parents and is attracting more pupils, it receives more money. Other factors, such as the size of the school premises or the number of children with special educational needs, may also be taken into consideration.

Governors are given full information about the costs of running their school and all other schools maintained by the LEA. Governors of primary and secondary schools with delegated budgets are responsible with the head teacher for:

—managing the school budget; and

—choosing the teaching and other staff.

The LEA, however, still employs the staff.

Audit and Inspection

The accounts of schools with delegated budgets are subject to regular audit. Internal auditors review financial management on behalf of the LEA. LEA external auditors are appointed by the Audit Commission; they ensure that LEAs have made proper arrangements to secure value for money. The head teacher has to consider and respond promptly to audit recommendations and report to the governing body on the results of the audit.

The Office for Standards in Education (OFSTED—see p. 29) has a statutory duty to inspect the way in which financial resources made available to schools are managed.

The Commission and the Office for Standards in Education have published a joint document, *Keeping Your Balance: Standards for Financial Administration in Schools*, for use by auditors and inspectors. It sets out the principles of good practice in financial administration and has been sent to all schools.

Self-governing Grant-maintained Schools

The 1988 legislation makes provision for LEA schools to become self-governing grant-maintained (GM) schools following assent by parents in a ballot. The school is no longer financed by the local education authority but by the Funding Agency for Schools.

Ballots

LEA schools are eligible to apply for GM status. An application has to be made to the Secretary of State, but this must be preceded by a ballot of parents at the school. The ballot must be held within the ten-week period following the decision by the school governing body to hold one.

A ballot can also be held without a resolution from the governing body if parents organise a written request to the governors, supported by a number of parents equal to at least 20 per cent of the number of pupils registered at the school. For example, if there are 1,000 pupils, a written request from 200 or more individual parents is sufficient for the ballot to take place. The ballot is held within ten weeks of the presentation of the request to the governing body.

Ballots are by post and are conducted by the Electoral Reform Society's company, Electoral Reform (Ballot Services) Ltd. Ballots conducted by anyone else are invalid. Ballot costs are met by the Government.

If a simple majority of voters favour GM status and if 50 per cent or more of those eligible have voted, the governors must prepare a formal application for GM status which is sent to the Secretary of State.

The ballot is disregarded if there is a tie or if less than 50 per cent of those eligible have voted. In these circumstances a second ballot must be held within 14 days of the first. The second ballot result is decisive, irrespective of the turnout. If there is a tie, there is no further ballot and proposals for GM status cannot be published.

Under the 1993 Education Act school governing bodies must consider each year whether to hold a parent's ballot on GM status. In their annual report to parents, governing bodies must say whether and when they have considered GM status since their last annual report and include details of their decisions. If they have decided not to hold a ballot, they must give reasons for this decision.

A Code of Practice agreed by the Government and the Society of Education Officers covers the information provided to parents by LEAs, the Government and the Grant-Maintained Schools Centre (see below) about GM status. It is designed to ensure that this is unbiased, factual, explanatory and non-party political in content, tone or presentation.

The Grant-Maintained Schools Centre, a company partly funded by the Department for Education, provides advice and information to anyone considering GM status and to those schools that have already achieved it.

Applications

If parents vote for GM status, the existing school governing body has to publish formal proposals within four months of the ballot result. The proposals have to be available for inspection either at the school or in some other local public building, such as the public library, or both. Once publication takes place, a copy must be sent to the Department for Education or the Welsh Office. There is a period of two months to allow time for any objections to the proposals to be made.

At the conclusion of this two-month period, the Secretary of State considers the proposals, taking into account any objections or comments that have been put forward. He or she may approve or reject the proposals or, after consulting the proposers, approve them with some changes such as a different start date. The Secretary of State can also ask the governing body to do more work on proposals he or she has rejected and to publish those revised proposals within a given time. Each application is decided on its merits and the school must show that it has a viable future as a GM school.

Small Schools

Under the 1993 Education Act small schools can choose GM status as part of a cluster of schools with a formal agreement to work together by sharing their resources and expertise. There are two forms of GM cluster—a joint scheme and a group. As with other schools wishing to become grant-maintained, both forms of cluster require support from parents in a ballot.

Under a joint scheme, schools appoint a joint committee to carry out certain functions while keeping their own governing bodies. The committee's functions must be agreed by all the governing bodies.

Schools wishing to go further than a joint scheme can come together in a group under a single governing body which is responsible for managing all the schools in the group, each school keeping its own individuality. The membership of the governing body is similar to that of an individual GM school, namely a mix of head teachers, appointed governors and elected parent-governors and teacher-governors.

New GM Schools

Under the 1993 Education Act, independent promoters and voluntary bodies will be able to publish proposals to set up new GM schools. In addition, independent schools will be able to become GM schools if they so wish. Once the proposals to set up a new GM school have been approved, the existing independent school is closed before the GM school opens.

Finance

Once a school becomes self-governing, maintenance grant from the Funding Agency for Schools is paid, based on the funding which it would have received had it remained under LEA control. The governors use this money to:

—pay the teachers and other staff;

—buy books, equipment and so on;

—pay for the upkeep of buildings; and

—provide services such as school meals for pupils and advisory support for teachers.

GM schools can also apply for capital grants to cover building work and for special purpose grants to help, for example, with in-service teacher training costs and capital expenditure. In order to ensure payment of grant, the school must be well managed and meet the general conditions of funding.

The Funding Agency is also responsible for financial monitoring of GM schools in England under regulations made by the Secretary of State. As the number of these schools increases, the Agency may take on some responsibility for securing enough school places in individual LEA areas. In areas where between 10 and 75 per cent of pupils are being educated in GM primary or secondary schools, the LEA and the Agency may both be responsible for this function. The Agency and not the LEA may be responsible for securing school places once 75 per cent or more of pupils are in GM schools. The Secretary of State has to make an Order before the Agency becomes responsible for providing school places.

In Wales there is a separate schools funding council with the same functions.

GM schools have to account for the way they spend public money by appointing auditors and publishing annual accounts. The audited accounts and other financial returns are sent to the Department for Education or the Welsh Office. Audited accounts are available at the annual parents' meeting and at the school for any member of the public to inspect.

School Characteristics
When schools publish their proposals for GM status, they cannot normally change their existing character. The only exception to this is a new facility under the 1993 Education Act designed to allow the school governors of a county school to propose a change in the school's character or to make its premises considerably larger if this is in order to fit in with LEA reorganisation plans.

Once GM status has been approved, a GM school may publish proposals to change its character, enlarge its premises or move the school to a new site. The Funding Agency for Schools is empowered to propose changes in GM schools in the areas where it is responsible for providing school places or jointly responsible for this with the LEA. Any school affected by such a proposal will be able to send a formal objection to the Secretary of State.

School Governors

GM schools have to provide a broad and balanced education for their pupils. The governors, including the head teacher, are responsible for drawing up the curriculum. The National Curriculum is provided, and daily collective worship and religious instruction follows the practice required of the school when it was under LEA control.

The school governing body consists of parents, teachers and people from the community served by the school. In the case of former voluntary schools which have a foundation or trust, the outside representation is provided by the foundation governors. At former county schools, it consists of a new category of 'first' governors who are appointed by the other governors as representatives of the local community. Some of the first governors must be members of the local business community.

Governing bodies are therefore made up as follows:

—five parent governors in secondary schools, or three to five parent governors in primary schools, elected by the parents of pupils at the school;

—at least one or two teacher governors, elected by the school's teachers;

—the head teacher; and

—a number of first or foundation governors (including at least two who are registered parents at the school) greater than the total of the other governors.

A GM secondary school may choose to include a new category of governor from the business community, known as sponsor governors. This step has to be approved by the Secretary of State. This approval may be sought as part of the process of becoming a GM school or may be obtained after the school has achieved GM status. A voluntary-aided school may also apply to take on sponsor governors. The governing body may include up to four sponsor governors.

Elected parent and teacher governors serve four-year terms and the other governors, including sponsor governors, serve for between five and seven years.

Role of LEAs

The role of the LEA will change as the number of GM schools increases. LEAs will retain responsibility for schools choosing not to become self-governing and will increasingly concentrate on functions such as:

—assessing pupils with special educational needs (see p. 7);

—providing support services;

—enforcing school attendance; and

—providing education for those pupils who cannot attend school.

City Technology Colleges

City Technology Colleges, launched in 1986, are independent schools created by a partnership of government and private sector sponsors. Their catchment areas cover deprived parts of the locality. The colleges teach the full National Curriculum, while emphasising technology and science. They do not charge fees and they aim to raise the general standard of education in their areas.

There are 15 colleges. Sponsors have contributed some £35 million to the schools and they remain closely involved in college government by bringing in business experience and expertise. Recurrent costs which are related to pupil numbers are met by the Government.

Colleges are legally bound to recruit their pupils across the full ability range. They have over 10,000 pupils and this number is expected to reach 15,000 when all the colleges reach full capacity. Colleges typically receive three applications for each pupil place.

The sponsors own or lease the schools and run them. They are responsible for employing teachers and other staff and make a substantial contribution towards the costs of buildings and equipment. There is no LEA involvement.

Technology Colleges
Under the 1993 Education Act secondary GM and voluntary-aided schools can apply to the Secretary of State to become technology colleges, which are designed to deliver the National Curriculum while placing a special emphasis on technology, science and mathematics. Applications are supported by business sponsors who have up to four representatives on the school governing body. Capital grants from public funds are available to complement business sponsorship. The colleges have to commit themselves to measurably higher levels of achievement in technology, science and maths.

The colleges will build on the achievements of the 15 city technology colleges (see p. 19) and on the teaching practices developed by the Technology Schools Initiative, which was launched by the Government in December 1991 to establish a network of secondary schools committed to providing technology and associated courses. Under the Initiative, government funds were allocated for capital spending on equipment and building work.

The National Curriculum and Assessment

Attendance at school in England and Wales has been compulsory since 1880, but the law has not, until recently, defined what pupils should be taught at school, with the exception of religious education. Demand for a more clearly defined curriculum grew over several decades, a turning point being a speech in 1976 by the then Prime Minister, James Callaghan, in which he referred to the strong case for a core curriculum of basic knowledge.

In recent years the Government has emphasised the need to improve the standards of education. This led to the 1988 Education Reform Act creating the National Curriculum, which is being introduced into state schools in England and Wales with the aim of achieving consistently high educational standards. The National Curriculum is a framework and not a detailed syllabus.

The Education Reform Act says that the school curriculum should:

—promote the spiritual, moral, cultural, mental and physical development of pupils at the school; and

—prepare pupils for the opportunities, responsibilities and experiences of adult life.

The legislation means that:

—a broad and balanced curriculum for each pupil is now established in law;

—this curriculum must be offered by all state schools and taken up fully by each pupil;

—the curriculum must promote development in all important areas of learning and experience; and

—the curriculum must serve to develop the pupil as an individual and a future adult member of the community.

The School Curriculum and Assessment Authority and the Curriculum and Assessment Authority for Wales are responsible for:

—keeping all aspects of the Curriculum and assessment arrangements under review and advising the Government;

—publishing and disseminating information related to the Curriculum, examinations and assessment;

—advising the Secretary of State on the recognition of qualifications or courses taught in schools; and

—advising on research and development.

Core and Other Subjects

The National Curriculum is made up of the core subjects of English, mathematics and science, and the following other subjects: technology (including information technology), history, geography, music, art, physical education and, for secondary school pupils, a modern foreign language. Secondary schools must offer at least one language of the European Union such as French, German or Spanish, although another modern language can be taken instead if the school is able to offer the choice. All these subjects must be taught, although schools are free to provide their teaching in a variety of ways.

In Wales the Welsh language is a National Curriculum core subject in Welsh-speaking schools and a foundation subject in other schools. Some 80 per cent of primary schools either use Welsh as a teaching medium or teach it as a second language. Nearly 90 per cent of secondary schools teach Welsh as a first or second language.

After the age of 14, art, music, history and geography are no longer compulsory, thereby giving pupils more choice over their studies. Most schools continue to offer these subjects and others that do not have to be studied under the National Curriculum, including a choice of job-related courses. Pupils have the right to advice about the choices that best suit their needs and parents have the right to be consulted about these.

Although not part of the National Curriculum, religious education is compulsory in all state schools. Locally agreed syllabuses, which have to be reviewed regularly, emphasise Christianity while taking account of the teaching and practices of other principal religions. Parents can withdraw their children from religious education classes.

Under provisions of the 1993 Education Act, which amend previous legislation and which enter into force in September 1994, state secondary schools are required to make provision for sex education for all pupils registered at the school. This includes education about HIV and AIDS and other sexually transmitted diseases. In state primary schools the governing body is responsible for considering whether sex education should be offered to their pupils.

In all state schools any sex education must encourage young people to have regard to moral considerations and the value of family life. Parents are entitled to withdraw their children from all or part of sex education classes other than certain elements in the National Curriculum Science Order. All state schools must publish in their prospectus a summary of the content and organisation of any sex education they provide. The school governing body must keep, and make available to parents on request, a written statement of its sex education policy.

Key Stages

The National Curriculum is divided into four sections, known as key stages.

—Key Stage 1 for ages 5 to 7;

—Key Stage 2 for ages 7 to 11;

—Key Stage 3 for ages 11 to 14; and

—Key Stage 4 for ages 14 to 16.

National Curriculum Subject Orders

Under the 1988 Act, Parliamentary Orders for each National Curriculum subject set out programmes of study, i.e. the subject matter to be taught. The Orders also cover attainment targets (the knowledge, skills and understanding to be acquired by pupils during their school career). Teachers can use the study programmes to construct their schemes of work in the classroom.

There is a system of grading for each attainment target, this taking the form of a ten-level scale. Different children move at different speeds up the scale and the same child may move more quickly in some subjects than others.

Assessment

The aim of the national assessment system is to:

—help raise expectations;

—define standards; and

—provide information for parents about their children's progress.

Confined to the core subjects of English, maths and science at key stages 1, 2 and 3, the process is a combination of national tests and assessment by teachers. In addition, pupils in Wales are also assessed in Welsh. Teacher assessments and test results are recorded separately and reported to parents. Teacher assessment continues throughout each key stage. National Curriculum tests are taken at the end of the key stage and test skills and understanding built up throughout this period.

The main vehicle for assessing 16-year-olds in the National Curriculum subjects is the General Certificate of Secondary Education (GCSE) examination, which is a combination of written papers and classroom assessment.

The Dearing Reviews

In response to concern expressed about excessive bureaucracy and curriculum overload, the Government took action in April 1993 by inviting Sir Ron Dearing, then Chairman designate of the School Curriculum and Assessment Authority, to review the National Curriculum and its assessment arrangements. The Curriculum Council for Wales was involved in a similar review of the Curriculum for Wales.

Sir Ron initiated a wide-ranging consultation, seeking the views of teachers, head teachers, subject specialists, industry, parents and others concerned with education. In the light of this he produced Interim and Final reports in July and December 1993 which recommended that:

—the existing National Curriculum for 5–14 year olds should be streamlined to release one day a week for schools to use at their own discretion;

—the reduction in Curriculum content for this age group should be concentrated outside the core subjects of English, maths and science while leaving intact in every subject an unchanged kernel of ground to be covered;

—flexibility within the Curriculum for 14–16 year olds should be increased to allow schools a wider range of academic and vocational options;

—teachers' workload should be cut through simplification of the National Curriculum and reduced testing and recording demands;

—a simplified ten level scale should be kept and run only to key stage 3; and

—all subjects should be reviewed simultaneously and then remain unchanged for five years.

These recommendations were accepted by the Government.

In January 1994 the School Curriculum and Assessment Authority undertook a comprehensive review of all National Curriculum subjects and in May 1994 draft proposals for each of these were issued for public consultation in England. This consultation involved over 30,000 addressees and sought the views of all concerned with education. The new National Curriculum Orders are due to become law by the end of 1994; they will come into force in schools in September 1995 for key stages 1, 2 and 3, (see p.24) and in September 1996 for key stage 4.

The 5–14 age group will continue to study the core subjects and the other National Curriculum subjects, but the time devoted to the mandatory Curriculum will be cut by 20 per cent in accordance with Sir Ron's recommendations.

Pupils between the ages of 14 and 16 will be required to study English, mathematics and science, together with physical education, religious education and sex education. From 1996, they will also be required to study at least short courses in technology and a modern foreign language. This will leave up to 40 per cent of curriculum time available for schools to offer pupils a wide range of academic and vocational courses tailored to their individual abilities and aptitudes.

As well as the existing choice of courses, there will be a pilot in 1995 of new vocational courses occupying half the time of a full General National Vocational Qualifications course[2] and aimed at the 14–16 age group.

The Curriculum in Wales

Similar developments are taking place in Wales in the light of advice from the Curriculum Council for Wales and Sir Ron Dearing. For 5–14 year olds the same range of subjects in the National Curriculum will be maintained, including Welsh as a first and second language, and the time devoted to the mandatory curriculum will be cut by 20 per cent. The mandatory curriculum for 14–16 year olds will be reduced to English, Welsh as a first language, mathematics, science, physical education, religious education and sex education. A wider range of vocational options will also be made available.

The statutory requirement for schools to provide Welsh as a second language is being suspended from September 1994; this will

---

[2] The GNVQ is a vocational alternative to GCSEs and the Advanced level of the General Certificate of Education.

be reviewed in good time for it to be reintroduced as a mandatory subject in 1999 if schools are demonstrating satisfactory progress in introducing the subject. In the meantime, schools will be encouraged to carry on teaching Welsh as a second language for 14–16 year olds and the Welsh Office will continue to invest substantially in in-service training and other measures needed to secure its successful re-introduction as a statutory requirement.

The new Curriculum and Assessment Authority for Wales was established in April 1994 and replaced the Curriculum Council for Wales.

Qualifications for 16-year-olds

Qualifications for 16-year-old pupils are approved by the Secretary of State acting on advice from the School Curriculum and Assessment Authority and its Welsh equivalent. They must have suitable certification and reporting arrangements and be authenticated by a competent body. The Authority considers and approves syllabuses leading to approved qualifications.

Monitoring

Examining bodies must make sure that their examinations are of good quality. The School Curriculum and Assessment Authority monitors and evaluates a sample of examinations each year through scrutinies carried out by teams of independent experts with experience of teaching and examining in the subject. The aim of the scrutinies is to ensure that examinations are fair and effective. Teams analyse written information about an examination, including syllabuses, question papers, marking schemes, scripts and statistics; they also observe the main examining processes. Scrutiny reports, containing recommendations for improving the examination, are checked by the relevant Authority subject committee and sent to the Authority. The examining body has to respond to the recommendations and satisfy the Authority that appropriate action has been taken.

There is a mandatory Code of Practice which has been endorsed by the Government as the basis for the future conduct of the GCSE examination. Compliance with the Code is a requirement for the approval of GCSE qualifications and associated syllabuses. The aim of the Code is to ensure:

—quality and consistency in the examining process across all examining groups offering GCSEs; and

—consistency in each subject across different examining bodies and different syllabuses and from year to year.

The Independent Appeals Authority for School Examinations hears appeals, made in writing, against grades awarded in GCSE examinations. It only hears an appeal when the processes of the examining body concerned are exhausted. The aim is to ensure that candidates who use the school examination system, and their parents and schools, are satisfied that grades awarded are as fair and accurate as they can be.

Educational Standards

School Inspections

The Office for Standards in Education (OFSTED) is responsible for school inspection in England. Under 1992 legislation, it keeps the Secretary of State for Education informed about:

—the quality of education provided by schools;

—the educational standards achieved in those schools;

—schools' financial efficiency; and

—the spiritual, moral, social and cultural development of pupils.

The Secretary of State can request advice from OFSTED on issues relating to quality and standards in education.

OFSTED recruits, trains and registers suitable applicants for the status of registered inspector, entitled to lead an inspection team and co-ordinate inspections. In addition it recruits and trains the other members of the teams, including lay inspectors. Some training is being devolved to accredited independent trainers. However, OFSTED retains responsibility for the design of courses, the materials used in them and the assessment of trainees. Independent inspectors work under contract and the work they obtain depends on the outcome of competitive bidding.

OFSTED's professional staff—Her Majesty's Inspectors (HMIs)—continue to report to the Secretary of State on specific issues or areas of school education and undertake a wide range of other inspection work.

In Wales the Office of Her Majesty's Chief Inspector of Schools is responsible for inspections.

Inspection Cycle

At least two tenders from registered inspectors are sought by OFSTED for each inspection, the aim being to achieve best value for money. Schools are inspected every four years to identify their strengths and weaknesses in order to improve the quality of education offered and raise standards achieved by pupils. Copies of inspection reports are published and a summary given to the parents of the children in the school.

The first inspections under the new system started in September 1993 for secondary schools and will begin in September 1994 for primary and special schools.

In Wales schools are inspected every five years.

Inspection Teams

The registered inspector seeking a contract has to demonstrate that the inspection team is sufficient and competent to conduct the inspection and that all team members are trained. Teams inspecting secondary schools must contain a balance of subject specialists and those competent to inspect the broader aspects of school education. If a school has pupils with special educational needs, the team must contain inspectors able to inspect the provision made for these pupils. Each team must have at least one lay inspector without personal experience of school management or the provision of education in any school, except in a voluntary capacity such as a school governor.

The lay inspector is there to provide a 'common sense' view from someone who is not professionally involved in education.

OFSTED is responsible for monitoring registered inspectors' work. It:

—checks reports and summaries;

—scrutinises them against the inspection evidence on which they are based; and

—observes registered inspectors at work from time to time.

OFSTED requires all registered inspectors to adhere to a document setting out the standards for inspection, criteria for judgment and the practices to be followed.

Inspection Process

A meeting is arranged between the inspector and parents of registered pupils at the school before the inspection, in order to provide an opportunity for parents to express their views to the inspectors.

When an inspection gets under way, the classes seen have to be representative of all age and ability groups. Work must be seen in all National Curriculum and other subjects included in the inspection specification.

If the registered inspector concludes that the school is failing, or is likely to fail, to give its pupils an acceptable standard of education, he or she must express that opinion in the report.

Once the inspection is concluded, the registered inspector is expected to offer to discuss the main findings with the school governing body and separately with the head teacher and other senior members of the school management team as soon as possible. This provides an opportunity to check on matters of factual accuracy.

Final Reports

An inspection report should include:

—basic information about the school, including the intake of pupils and the area served by it, the number of pupils and teachers, the pupil-teacher ratio, average class size in primary schools, average teaching group size in secondary schools and truancy records;

—a summary of standards of pupils' achievements in National Curriculum and other subjects;

—comments about pupils' competence in basic skills;

Children at the Turney School, South London, with their reading folders. Special schools follow the National Curriculum at a pace adapted to the needs of the children.

Schools are encouraged to develop the teaching of technological subjects. Here a pupil operates a pillar drill, constructing a model windmill.

A GCSE examination at Islington Green comprehensive school. In 1991–92 just over a half of all school leavers in Great Britain obtained a GCSE grade A to C (or equivalent pass) in English and 40 per cent in mathematics.

Starting off the school day with morning assembly at Hounslow Heath Junior School.

A student teacher from the London Institute of Education taking part in school-based training.

The National Curriculum is not the whole curriculum: a drama class encourages pupils' wider interests.

Northern Ireland Centre for Learning Resources

School computers at St Mary's secondary school in Irvinestown, Northern Ireland, enable pupils to master the use of information technology.

Protestant and Roman Catholic children are taught together in an integrated primary school in County Antrim, Northern Ireland.

—key points for action regarding the quality of learning;

—an evaluation of the extent to which the school uses its resources efficiently;

— a statement about the overall quality of pupils' behaviour;

—an evaluation of pupils' spiritual, moral, social and cultural development;

—a clear statement about the quality of teaching;

—a view on the effectiveness, accuracy and consistency of the assessment of pupils' work and the usefulness of reports issued to parents;

—comments on the quality, range and organisation of the curriculum, including the ability to meet the requirements of the National Curriculum; and

—information about standards achieved by pupils with special educational needs.

The report should also contain information about:

—the school's policy for equal opportunities;

—the quality of the school's management; and

—the deployment of staff.

In addition, the inspection report should include a judgment about the effectiveness of school arrangements for supporting and guiding individual pupils and for monitoring and recording their progress.

Failing Schools

The 1993 Education Act contains measures designed to deal with failing schools. The Government expects Her Majesty's Chief Inspector to arrange for the inspection of schools likely to be at risk.

Under the Act, OFSTED and its Welsh equivalent notify the appropriate Secretary of State of any school at risk. The governing body is required to draw up an action plan and the LEA has to submit to the Secretary of State a copy of the plan and a commentary on it, together with a statement of any action it plans to take.

If the Secretary of State is satisfied with the proposed course of action, he allows the governing body and the LEA time to remedy the problems identified in the inspection report. In the case of county, voluntary controlled or maintained special schools, the LEA is able to appoint new governors and withdraw financial delegation. The power to appoint additional governors is exercised by the foundation of a voluntary aided school. If it becomes clear that the plan is not working, the Secretary of State can replace the governing body by putting the school under the management of an Education Association (EA). He can also exercise this power if he judges that the action plan from the governing body and support from the LEA is insufficient to improve the performance of the school.

The EA is a small, cohesive body consisting of a chairperson and not less than four other members. It has the same powers and receives the same funding as the governing body of a self-governing school. An EA can be in charge of more than one failing school.

The Secretary of State has the power to provide the EA with a remit to improve each school under its management. The EA's job is to tackle the problems of a school, revitalise its management and, if necessary, make staffing changes. The EA benefits from advice from parents, business, industry and other interested parties. It replaces the existing governing body, which is disbanded, and the LEA's duty to maintain the school ceases.

Once the school is turned around, it normally moves on to become a self-governing grant-maintained (GM) school.

The Act provides parallel measures for dealing with failing GM schools. The Secretary of State has powers to appoint additional governors or replace any or all of the first governors if an inspection identifies the school as failing.

Teachers

Steps have been taken to reform the teacher training system in order to improve the quality of the teaching profession.

Almost all teachers in publicly-funded schools have to complete a recognised course of initial teacher training. Graduates can obtain qualified teacher status by successfully completing a one-year Postgraduate Certificate of Education (PGCE) course. Non-graduates usually qualify by taking a four-year Bachelor of Education (B.Ed) honours degree course.

A number of consortia of schools provide their own courses of initial teacher training for postgraduates which lead to Qualified Teacher Status.

Secondary Schools
In order to improve the quality of teaching, schools are playing a much larger part in initial teacher training as full partners of higher education institutions. Under new criteria for secondary schools coming into force between September 1992 and September 1994,

the amount of time spent by students in schools during teacher training is being increased.

The criteria stipulate that students should have knowledge and understanding of the requirements of the National Curriculum for their specialist subjects . Students are also expected to be aware of current statutory reporting arrangements and will be given some opportunity to demonstrate ability in reporting and discussing pupils' progress with parents. In addition, students have to show the ability to conduct assessments of pupils in line with the National Curriculum.

Primary Schools

Reforms are taking place in initial teacher training courses for primary school teachers. These come into effect for new courses from September 1994 and for all courses by September 1996.

They include:

—new criteria for training courses, focusing on subject knowledge and the skills needed for effective classroom teaching;

—more training in schools to enable students to develop and apply practical teaching skills; and

—continuing study in higher education institutions of subject knowledge necessary for sound teaching of the National Curriculum.

The reforms also involve greater diversity of courses, including:

— a new three-year, six-subject B.Ed designed to prepare teachers for work across the primary curriculum; and

—courses preparing teachers for work as subject specialists at key stage 2 of the National Curriculum.

In-service Training

Schools have greater freedom to manage budgets for in-service teacher training and to decide which members of staff should benefit. Funding comes largely from the Government's Grants for Education Support and Training Scheme, which helps schools implement major educational reforms such as implementation of the National Curriculum and local financial management. Separate funding is available for self-managed schools.

Teacher Training Agency

From 1995–96 the Teacher Training Agency established under the 1994 Education Act will finance initial teacher training courses, ensure that national standards are met and promote teaching as a career. The Agency's objectives include:

—helping to raise teaching standards;

—improving the quality and efficiency of all routes into the teaching profession; and

—securing the involvement of schools in all training courses.

Schools will take on more responsibility for planning and managing courses and for the selection, training and assessment of students, usually in partnership with institutions. They will train students to teach their specialist subjects, to assess pupils and to manage classes; they will also supervise students and assess their competence.

If they wish to do so, consortia of schools will be able to run courses for postgraduate students. Other courses, including all undergraduate courses, will be run by universities and colleges in partnership with schools.

The new Agency will fund teacher training institutions in England; the Welsh Higher Education Funding Council will carry out parallel duties in Wales.

Teacher Appraisal

There is a two-year appraisal cycle for serving teachers. The first part of the appraisal consists of classroom observation, an appraisal interview and the preparation of an appraisal statement, including targets for future action. In the second year, a follow-up meeting takes place to review progress and targets.

Complaints Procedure

Complaints about the way schools are run are best handled locally and informally. If it proves impossible for the parties concerned to reach an agreement on how to put things right, the 1988 Education Reform Act provides for LEAs to set up a statutory complaints procedure approved by the Secretary of State. This deals with complaints against the actions of the LEA or a school governing body.

As a last resort, a complainant can go to the Secretary of State if he or she thinks that the LEA or the governing body has acted unreasonably or has failed to carry out its duties. After considering the case, the Secretary of State may direct the LEA or the governing body to remedy matters.

Complaints about teaching are treated as complaints against the school governing body. The arrangements do not apply to complaints about the actions of individual teachers or the head teacher.

Scotland

Overall education policy is the responsibility of the Scottish Office Education Department. Delivery of the service is entrusted to the twelve Regional and Island education authorities. The Secretary of State for Scotland has ministerial responsibility.

Most schools supported from public funds are provided by education authorities and are known as public schools.

Parental Rights

Choosing a School

Parents have a right to a free school place for their children from the age of 5 to 16. Under 1981 legislation, they also have the right to nominate a school they wish their child to attend. They may enrol their child in the local school in the catchment area in which they live or they may put forward a placement request for another school for their child. Since 1982 well over 200,000 placement requests (90 per cent) have been granted.

An authority can only refuse such a request if a school is already full. If there are more requests for a school than there are places, each local authority must produce guidelines to be followed in deciding who should be accepted. Normally, first places are given to children living within the school's catchment area and preference may be given to those who have brothers or sisters at the school. In the case of secondary schools, first places are generally also given to children coming from associated primary schools.

If parents are unhappy with the authority's decision on a placing request, they can appeal to a committee which must be set up by the education authority. It has no more than seven members, who may be members of the authority or regional councillors or local people such as teachers and parents who are unconnected with the school concerned.

If the appeal committee agrees with the refusal to place a child in the school wanted by the parents, an appeal can be made to the sheriff whose judgment is final.

Information about Schools

Each school publishes a school handbook which informs parents about the organisation of the school and what is taught. Policies regarding discipline, school uniform and other issues are also described.

More information is being provided under the Parents' Charter. All schools are obliged to publish more details about subjects taught in the school and what the curriculum aims to do. In addition, they are expected to publish:

—results in public examinations, set out in a standard way so that it is easier to make comparisons;

—details about the destinations of school leavers;

—levels of attendance and truancy; and

—the costs of running the school.

School reports must:

—tell parents about their child's academic performance and general development;

—include the results of national tests;

—help parents to judge their child's performance against that of other children of the same age; and

—give parents the chance to respond to the report by discussing it with the teachers concerned.

Parents also have the right to see the records kept by the school on their child.

Special Educational Needs

If parents have a child with special educational needs arising from disability or learning difficulties, experts can be called in to make a full assessment of these needs. Parents have a right to be involved at all stages. The initial assessment may lead to a Record of Needs being drawn up; this will set out the help the child requires and name the school which the pupil should attend.

A Record of Needs may state that the child should be educated in a special school. Parents of a child with a Record of Needs have the right to make a placing request for a school of their choice and may also nominate an independent or grant-aided special school. In such cases the education authority pays all the necessary costs of special education, including school fees if charged.

School Boards

Education authorities are required to establish school boards, which play a significant part in the administration and management of schools. Although membership of each board varies according to the size of the school, there must be a majority of parent members, with the balance made up from teacher members and co-opted members. In this way, parents are encouraged to have a much closer involvement in the work of the school and better links can be forged between home, school and local community.

Devolved Management

The Government has requested education authorities to bring forward schemes for devolved school management. Under these at least 80 per cent of school running costs would be devolved, including teaching and non-teaching staff costs. Financial allocations to schools would be based predominantly on pupil numbers. Schools would have more freedom to choose their providers of supplies and services. The guidelines state that education authorities should consult head teachers, school staff, school boards and parents about the formulation and operation of schemes for their areas.

It is hoped that devolved management will cover all primary and secondary schools by April 1996.

Self-governing Schools

Under legislation passed in 1989, schools managed by local authorities have the right to seek self-governing status, provided that there is a school board in place to run the school.

Before any application is made to the Secretary of State, a ballot of parents must be called by the school board or a significant group of parents. A secret postal ballot must then be conducted by the Electoral Reform Society. If a ballot result shows that fewer than half the parents eligible to vote have done so, a second and decisive ballot must be held within 14 days.

If a majority of parents approves the change, the school board puts forward proposals for self-government to the Secretary of State for a decision. He or she may approve the proposals as submitted, reject the proposals or approve the proposals with modifications, having first consulted the school board and the education authority.

Once the school becomes self-governing, the school board is replaced by a board of management which comprises:

—a majority of parent members, elected from and by parents;

—members elected from and by teachers and instructors at the school;

—members appointed by the board itself; and

—the head teacher.

The board of management employs staff, is responsible for school premises and enters into contracts.

Self-governing schools are funded by the Scottish Office Education Department.

Curriculum and Assessment

The content and management of the school curriculum are the responsibility of education authorities and head teachers, although authoritative guidance is provided by the Secretary of State.

National Curricular Framework

In order to ensure an overall pattern for school education, education authorities and most independent schools have agreed to work within a national curricular framework. The Secretary of State, bearing in mind any advice given by the Scottish Consultative Council on the Curriculum, adjusts this framework from time to time to ensure that it is in tune with changes in society and the economy. Within the framework, each school works out programmes and selects courses suited to the needs of its own pupils and the local community.

During the years between 5 and 12 teaching and learning is organised by class teachers within five broad areas. These are:

—language, which involves talking and listening, reading and writing;

—mathematics, that is, solving practical problems by counting, measuring, using symbols, shapes and patterns and by handling data;

—environmental studies, which means applying elements of geography, history, health, science and technology to practical situations, projects and themes;

—expressive arts, involving the exploration of aspects of art, music, drama and physical education; and

—religious and moral education, in which pupils learn about themselves, religious beliefs and living with others.

The national framework suggests minimum percentages of time for each of these main areas so that there is a proper balance between them. Some 20 per cent of time is left to schools' discretion in order to allow them to make adjustments as children progress through the school and as individual needs arise and change.

During the six years of secondary education for pupils aged 12 to 18, most teachers are subject specialists. To assist schools in making sure that all pupils have a broad and balanced education during their secondary years, the national curricular framework recommends that schools should organise their curriculum within a number of modes which replace the five primary curricular areas. These are:

—mathematical studies and applications;

—scientific studies and applications;

—language and communication;

—social and environmental studies;

—technological activities and applications;

—creative and aesthetic activities;

—physical education; and

—religious and moral education.

All pupils between 12 and 16 study at least one course related to each mode. Within the language and communication mode, for instance, all pupils are expected to study English and another language. For most modes there are several courses to choose from. As an example, biology, chemistry, physics, general science, electronics and geology can contribute to the scientific studies made. All schools must include maths and science at this stage of the curriculum.

Between the ages of 16 and 18, pupils continue to follow a curriculum based on these modes but do not normally cover all of them. Careers education and work experience help prepare pupils for the move from school to training, post–school education or jobs.

Assessment and Reporting

For pupils between the ages of 5 and 14, guidelines cover descriptions of competencies in each area and attainment targets. Their purpose is to enable schools and teachers to structure their curriculum and take decisions about the progress of individual pupils on a basis which can be easily understood and interpreted.

Guidance to schools on assessment and reporting to parents stresses the need for systematic assessment by teachers of pupils; it also provides a framework for full and effective reporting to parents.

New arrangements for the national testing of primary school pupils started in January 1993 and operate in the first two years of secondary schooling from January 1994.

Teachers report on pupils' learning and attainment of targets across the curriculum using their professional judgment and the evidence available to them from their own continuous assessment throughout the year. The national tests in reading, writing and mathematics are part of this process and are designed to provide evidence of attainment by pupils.

The basic principles underpinning the system of national tests are that:

—arrangements apply to all pupils;

—the tests assess pupils' progress against nationally agreed attainment targets;

—the tests, based on materials produced by teachers, should be part of teachers' continuous assessment of pupils' progress;

—a pupil is tested in an aspect of reading, writing and mathematics when the teacher's own assessment indicates that the pupil has largely achieved attainment targets at one level in that aspect and is ready to move from that level to the next;

—tests are selected, administered and marked by teachers themselves; and

—details of an individual pupil's performance in tests is given only to the pupil and parent and recorded in the pupil's progress record.

The skills and processes included in the tests are limited to those that can be assessed using relatively short paper-based tasks. Others are assessed by the teacher during class work. Schools are given flexibility in the choice of content, application and timing, consistent with an effective system of testing which does not put pupils under undue pressure.

The test consists of a series of test units. A reading test, for instance, consists of two units—narrative reading and reading for information—each of which takes 20 to 25 minutes to complete. The mathematics test has four units, each taking 15 to 20 minutes to complete. Each unit has a detailed marking scheme and a teacher's guide.

A selection of units in both language and mathematics is available in Gaelic.

Schools choose test items from a catalogue issued by the 5–14 Assessment Unit of the Scottish Examination Board, which also provides advice to teachers on how to plan and give tests.

Education authorities are responsible for ensuring that testing takes place. The Assessment Unit monitors standards each year by taking a sample of marked tests.

Test results are not used to place individual pupils in rank order in their class, to select pupils for particular schools or to place schools in any sort of rank order.

In the third and fourth years of secondary education pupils take a number of two-year Standard Grade courses of the Scottish Certificate of Education and may also take short courses and modules. These are assessed and certificated by the Scottish Examination Board or by the Scottish Vocational Education Council.

Educational Standards

All schools are being required to produce a document setting out their educational plans and targets for the two years ahead, with a report on progress over the previous two years.

School Inspections

The Parents' Charter in Scotland stresses the need for independent inspections in order to assure quality of school education. The Inspectorate is entrusted with the task of making frank and clear assessments of the strengths and weaknesses in schools, in teaching and learning, in attainment, in aspects of the curriculum and in school management. The first priority of the reports is to assess the standards being achieved and the arrangements made to improve and monitor them.

Her Majesty's Inspectors are independent of the education authorities and are accountable to the Secretary of State. The Senior Chief Inspector has direct access to the Secretary of State, enabling him to provide frank and objective advice independent of the Scottish Office Education Department.

A target number of school inspections to be completed each year is fixed by the Secretary of State.

Steps are being taken to recruit as inspectors people who have substantive and relevant experience beyond education and to involve lay people in inspections; the aim is to have lay participation in all inspection teams from school session 1994–95.

More Openness

In order to further the aims of the Parents' Charter, the conduct and outcome of inspections are being made more public and open. Under these new arrangements, there is discussion with the school board early in each inspection so that the views of parents are ascertained and can be taken fully into account in the inspection. Local business people are being given the opportunity to offer inspectors their views in advance and are given copies of the relevant inspection report. A full report on each inspection is published and a short summary given to parents showing the school's strengths and weaknesses. Inspection reports state how well pupils and schools are doing and identify good practice as well as assess value for money. If inspectors find that school performance is not good enough, they say so.

Parents are also told about action to be taken to tackle the recommendations of the report. There is a follow-up inspection about a year later to assess and confirm progress in remedying any weaknesses identified in the first report.

Inspectors also publish guidance on how they assess the quality of education in a school. This is designed to help parents, the school and the local education authority to judge how well the school is doing.

The Inspectorate's Audit Unit is responsible for monitoring the performance of all schools through scrutiny of school development plans, examination results, attendance and truancy figures and the destination of school leavers. The Unit identifies elements requiring attention and improvement in individual schools and in the system as a whole.

Inspectorate findings from school inspections in 1991–92 gave an overall picture of an education service in which much is of good quality or better. It did, however, highlight a number of important areas requiring attention in a significant number of schools.

Quality of Teaching

Since 1987 the Scottish teaching profession has been all-graduate in order to ensure that pupils are taught by qualified and professionally competent staff. Teachers of academic subjects in secondary schools must hold a degree containing passes in the subjects they teach.

Action has been taken to improve the standard of teacher training courses. All new pre-service and major in-service courses provided by teacher training institutions must be approved by the Scottish Office Education Department and a validating body.

In order to maintain and improve the quality of teachers, the Government introduced a system of staff development and appraisal in 1992. Teachers' work is assessed at least once every two years. Detailed guidance is given to education authorities about how this should be done. There are procedures for action in cases where a teacher's performance is clearly unsatisfactory.

All Scottish teachers have to be registered with the General Teaching Council (GTC) which:

—maintains a register of those eligible to teach in local education authority schools on successful completion of an approved teacher training course and a two-year probationary period;

—is responsible for a disciplinary procedure under which teachers guilty of professional misconduct may be removed permanently or temporarily from the register; and

—provides advice to the Secretary of State on teacher supply and the professional suitability of teacher training courses.

Complaints Procedure

Although schools and education authorities seek to give parents the best possible service, there are arrangements to deal with mistakes and omissions. The first point of contact is the head teacher, who parents can approach if they are unhappy with anything that happens to their child at school.

Northern Ireland

The Department of Education for Northern Ireland is responsible for the education system, which is administered by five education and library boards as the education authorities. The Secretary of State for Northern Ireland has overall ministerial responsibility.

The main categories of school supported by public funds are:

—controlled schools provided by the boards;

—maintained schools under overall general management from the Council for Catholic Maintained Schools;

—voluntary grammar schools, which may be under Roman Catholic management or non-denominational boards of governors; and

—grant-maintained integrated schools taking Protestant and Roman Catholic pupils.

Each school has a board of governors (see p. 54).

Parental Rights

Parents have the right to express a preference for the primary or secondary school they wish their children to attend, unless there are more children applying for places than the school has room for. In addition, a grammar school may decline to take a child if it thinks that the education it provides is inappropriate for the child.

A copy of the school's admissions criteria is supplied to parents. Only grammar schools may use academic ability as an admission criterion. In cases where schools are oversubscribed, children must be admitted on the basis of this admissions policy. For example, some schools give preference to those children who live near the school or to those who have a brother or sister already at the school.

If parents think that the admissions criteria have not been correctly applied, they can appeal against the school's decision to an independent tribunal established by the local education and library board. They have the right to present their case at the tribunal. If the tribunal finds in the parents' favour, the Board of Governors must admit the child to the school.

Recent legislation has provided for Protestant and Roman Catholic children to be educated together if parents so wish. Existing schools are able to become integrated schools and financial assistance is also available to parents wishing to set up new integrated schools.

Under the Parents' Charter for Northern Ireland, parents are entitled to:

—an annual report on their child's school performance;

—an annual report on the school from the Board of Governors;

—a prospectus about each individual school; and

—a publication by each education and library board about the education in its area.

The prospectus provides information about:

—the school's educational aims;

—the subjects and activities the school offers to pupils;

—arrangements for religious education and collective worship; and

—school policy on disciplinary matters.

Secondary schools must also provide information about public examinations and school examination results, pupil attendance rates and the destinations of pupils who leave the school. As soon as statutory assessment at the ages of 8, 11 and 14 begins, parents will have to be informed about the school's assessment results.

The Department of Education publishes information to enable parents to compare the performance of all primary, secondary and grammar schools. For secondary and grammar schools, this includes:

—each school's examination results;

—attendance rates at each school;

—the number of pupils who leave to go on to further or higher education; and

—the numbers in each school who leave to take up employment or training.

These tables are published in local newspapers and are available in local libraries.

When the statutory assessment system gets under way (see p. 58), the Department will publish information about each school's assessment results.

School Reports

Parents receive an annual report on their child's progress in school. It informs them about:

—the teacher's assessment of attainments in English, mathematics and science;

—progress in other subjects and school activities;

—their child's examination results;

—how the principal or class teacher sees their child's general progress;

—their child's attendance record; and

—arrangements for discussing the report with the teacher.

Local School Management

Schools are funded by a formula based on pupil numbers but which also takes into account factors such as the size of the school, accommodation costs and social and economic disadvantage. Each school receives an overall financial allocation for the board of governors to decide how to spend.

Boards of Governors

Each school has a Board of Governors which includes elected parent representatives. Parents have the right to vote in the election of these governors and to stand as a parent governor.

The Board of Governors is responsible for ensuring that the education provided at the school meets the requirements of the law. It also manages the school's finances and is responsible for employing teaching staff.

An annual report on the school's management must be provided to parents by the Board of Governors. It must tell parents about:

—procedures for the election of parent governors;

—how the Board of Governors has carried out its responsibilities regarding the curriculum and management of the school budget;

—the aims of the school and how far these have been achieved;

—the action taken to develop the school's links with the community; and

—how the Board of Governors promotes education for mutual understanding (see p. 57).

Parents must be invited by the Board of Governors to an annual meeting to discuss the report. If at least 10 per cent of the parents attend, they can put forward a resolution about the school or vote on resolutions put forward by other parents. The Board of Governors must consider and respond to any resolution supported by the majority of parents present at the meeting.

Curriculum and Assessment

The school curriculum for primary school children consists of five areas of study—English, mathematics, science and technology, the environment and society, and creative and expressive studies. The same areas apply to secondary school pupils together with a sixth, language studies.

The areas of study are made up of groups of subjects covering broad areas of the curriculum. Pupils have to follow programmes of study in certain subjects within each of the five or six areas during compulsory school education.

It is the intention that all primary school pupils will be taught the following subjects—English, mathematics, science, history, geography, physical education, art and design, technology and design, and music. Pupils aged 12 to 14 will study the same subjects, with the addition of a modern language. Those aged 15 and 16 must take English, mathematics and science and at least one subject from each of the three remaining areas of study.

These requirements are being introduced on a phased basis. However, changes are being made in the curriculum for primary school children following a review and advice received from the

Northern Ireland Council for the Curriculum, Examinations and Assessment (CCEA). As in England and Wales, the review was set up following concern about curriculum overload. The programmes of study will be revised and reduced in volume; the aim of the change is to ensure that schools can implement statutory requirements for most pupils in about 85 per cent of teaching time. This will leave 15 per cent of teaching time free for schools to give additional help with the basics for pupils who need it, to offer extra work to the most able pupils and to make room for school activities such as visits, sports events and concerts.

Programmes of study will be revised by working groups between September 1994 and February 1995. This will be followed by consultations with schools and final recommendations will be made in October 1995. The revised programmes of study will be implemented in September 1996.

Between September 1994 and September 1996 only the existing programmes of study for English, mathematics and science will continue to be a statutory requirement. Although schools will be required to teach all the other subjects of the primary curriculum, there will be no requirement to follow the programmes of study in these subjects.

In addition, programmes of study for 12 to 14 year olds will be reviewed and revised to take account of proposed changes for primary school children. This process will fit into the above timetable.

From the ages of 12 to 16 pupils must study at least one of five languages to fulfil statutory requirements. These languages are French, German, Italian, Spanish and Irish. Other languages may be studied in addition to one of the named five.

In addition, there are a number of themes which are included in the curriculum for all schools. They are not separate subjects but are woven through the main curriculum subjects. The themes are:

—cultural heritage;

—education for mutual understanding;

—health education;

—information technology;

—economic awareness; and

—careers education.

The first four of these are included in primary school curricula and all six in secondary curricula. The first of the themes is designed to help overcome distrust among the people of the province by enabling pupils to understand and evaluate the common experience of their cultural heritage; emphasis is also placed on the dependence of cultures on each other. The second theme is meant to teach pupils to understand other people's points of view and appreciate the benefits of resolving conflict by non-violent means.

The curriculum of every child must include religious education, although parents are free to withdraw their children from such classes. A compulsory core syllabus for religious education, drawn up by a group including representatives from the Roman Catholic and the main Protestant churches is being introduced into schools on a phased basis.

Education and library boards have a statutory responsibility to provide curriculum advice and support to all schools. In-service support for teachers is provided across all the areas of the curriculum. In addition, the Department of Education has introduced and increased minor works capital programmes to ensure that all schools have the necessary accommodation—particularly laboratories and workshops—to deliver the common curriculum to pupils.

The CCEA advises the Department of Education on the implementation of the common curriculum.

Assessment

Arrangements for statutory assessment of pupils are not yet in place. In the school year 1992–93 pilot assessments were organised for pupils at the ages of 11 and 14 who had followed programmes of study in English, mathematics and science for three years. A second pilot programme is taking place in 1993–94 covering pupils at the ages of 8, 11 and 14 and was substantially revised and simplified in the light of the first pilot. More pilot schemes will take place in the 1994–95 school year.

Assessment and attainment at the age of 16 will be measured by the General Certificate of Secondary Education (GCSE) examination or other public examinations of equivalent standard.

Standards of examinations are equivalent to those in England and Wales. The CCEA advises the Department of Education on assessment arrangements.

Schools for Pupils with Special Educational Needs

Education and library boards make provision for children with special educational needs in ordinary schools, special units attached to such schools or day or residential special schools.

The local board is responsible for carrying out formal assessments of such children's difficulties and it may decide that special educational provision is required. Details of this are set out in a statement given to parents, who are consulted about which school the child should attend. If parents are unhappy about the statement, they can appeal to the Department of Education.

The common curriculum is being introduced in special schools and units at the same time as in mainstream education. There is provision for the curriculum and assessment requirements to be modified to meet pupils' particular needs.

In May 1994 the Government announced proposals designed to improve provision for children with special educational needs. These follow the recent reforms in England and Wales (see p. 7) and include time limits for making assessments and statements, a Code of Practice for education and library boards and schools, and new rights for parents, including an independent tribunal to hear appeals on all aspects of the statementing process.

School Inspections

The Education and Training Inspectorate is the main source of advice and information to Ministers and officials. Its main functions are to:

— inspect, monitor and report on standards, trends and quality of provision throughout the education system and to advise the Department;

— seek to maintain and, where necessary, improve standards by identifying, evaluating and reporting on good practice and on weaknesses wherever these exist; and

— provide written reports for publication on what has been found by the inspection and the evaluation made by the inspector.

In 1993 the Government introduced a cycle and procedure for school inspections which means that every school will have a major inspection—general or focused—every five years. Before a general inspection takes place, parents are given the chance to talk to the inspection team about their views on the strengths and weaknesses of the school.

Parents receive a summary of the inspection report from the school. This outlines the strengths and weaknesses that have been identified and provides information about improvements that could be made. Parents also receive a copy of the Board of Governors' response to the report explaining how it intends to overcome any problems identified by the inspectors.

A copy of the inspection report on any school can be obtained from the Inspectorate Support Branch of the Department of Education.

Complaints Procedure

If parents have a complaint to make about the school, the curriculum or the teaching staff, contact is first made with the school principal (the head teacher). Most problems are resolved after discussion with the principal or the class teacher. Parents can also ask the Board of Governors to consider the matter.

There are independent tribunals which deal with unresolved complaints. These cover the school curriculum, pupil expulsions and the statement drawn up for pupils with special educational needs.

If a parent thinks that the result received in a child's examination is wrong, he or she can ask the Northern Ireland Council for the Curriculum, Examinations and Assessment to review the matter. The Council can recheck the grade received and, if necessary, arrange to re-mark the examination papers. If parents remain dissatisfied, they can appeal to the Independent Appeals Authority on School Examinations, in London (see p. 29).

Addresses

Audit Commission, 1 Vincent Square, London SW1P 2PN.

Department for Education, Sanctuary Buildings, Great Smith Street, London SW1P 3BT.

Department of Education for Northern Ireland, Rathgael House, Balloo Road, Bangor, County Down BT12 2PR.

General Teaching Council for Scotland, 5 Royal Terrace, Edinburgh EH7 5AF.

Independent Appeals Authority for School Examinations, Newcombe House, 45 Notting Hill Gate, London W11 3JB.

Office for Standards in Education (OFSTED), Elizabeth House, York Road, London SE1 7PH.

Office of Her Majesty's Chief Inspector of Schools in Wales, Phase 2, Government Buildings, Ty Glas Road, Llanishen, Cardiff CF4 5WE.

School Curriculum and Assessment Authority, Newcombe House, 45 Notting Hill Gate, London W11 3JB.

Scottish Consultative Council on the Curriculum, Gardyne Road, Dundee DD5 1NY.

Scottish Examination Board, Ironmills Road, Dalkeith EH22 1LE.

The Scottish Office Information Directorate, New St Andrew's House, Edinburgh EH1 3TG.

Welsh Office Information Division, Cathays Park, Cardiff CF1 3NQ.

Further Reading

			£
Choice and Diversity: A New Framework for Schools. Cm 2021. ISBN 0 10 120212 1.	HMSO	1992	8.60
The Government's Expenditure Plans 1993–94 to 1995–96. Cm 2210. ISBN 0 10 122102 9. Department for Education.	HMSO	1993	8.75
The Handbook for the Inspection of Schools. ISBN 0 11 350017 3.	HMSO	1993	15.00
How to Become a Grant-Maintained School	Department for Education	1993	Free
The National Curriculum and its Assessment: An Interim Report (the Dearing Report).	School Curriculum and Assessment Authority	1993	Free
The National Curriculum and its Assessment (Final Dearing Report).	School Curriculum and Assessment Authority	1994	Free

Index

Printed in the United Kingdom for HMSO.
Dd.297712, 9/94, C30, 56-6734, 5673.